AGILITY

OVER 50

About the Author

Dr. Bridget Tarkington, Ph.D., is a strategist, technologist, and leadership advisor with more than 25 years of experience in technology, program management, and organizational leadership. Her work has focused on helping complex systems—teams, platforms, and leaders—adapt under pressure while preserving coherence, values, and direction.

Her understanding of agility does not come from dating theory. It comes from decades spent operating in environments where adaptability was essential, accountability was measurable, and failure to respond accurately carried real consequences. In those spaces, clarity was not optional, and endurance without adjustment was never mistaken for strength.

Over time, she recognized a powerful parallel: Relationships function like systems. What sustains them is not intention or longevity but responsiveness, alignment, and a willingness to act on reality rather than on narrative.

Rigid systems fail. So do rigid relational frameworks that reward endurance over discernment.

Agility Over 50 combines professional insight with lived experience, offering a grounded, unsentimental perspective on relationships, autonomy, and self-leadership in later life. The book applies the same principles trusted in high-stakes leadership environments—pattern recognition, course correction, and the protection of core values—to the emotional and relational decisions that women are often taught to endure rather than evaluate.

Dr. Tarkington lives and works by the principles this book embodies: clarity over performance, alignment over accommodation, and movement guided by self-respect rather than urgency.

AGILITY
OVER 50

Elevate, Shift, and Renew
The Mindset of Dating

Dr. Bridget Tarkington, Ph.D.

Published by Agility Press

ISBN: 979-8-9945398-0-4 E-Book
ISBN: 979-8-9945398-1-1 Paperback
ISBN: 979-8-9945398-2-8 Hardback
Printed in the United States of America

This book is for informational and educational purposes only. It does not constitute medical, psychological, or legal advice.

Agility

She did not harden.
She clarified.

She learned the difference
between waiting and listening,
between patience and postponement,
between effort and alignment.

She stopped mistaking urgency for truth
and intensity for depth.
She let time reveal what words could not.

What stayed did not require persuasion.
What left did not require chasing.

She became still enough
to notice what cost her peace—
and strong enough
to stop paying it.

This is not retreat.
This is refinement.

She is not closed.

She is complete.

And from that place,

whatever arrives

must arrive aligned—

or not at all.

Contents

Acknowledgements

This book bears the imprint of three generations. My grandmother taught me, gently and consistently, that dignity is not negotiable. She modeled self-respect without performance and strength without justification. She learned early that clarity is a form of kindness, and that patience should never require self-erasure. Much of what I know about discernment, I learned by watching how she moved through the world without apology.

My mother instilled resilience, responsibility, and the expectation that women think for themselves. She taught me that independence is not isolation and that competence is a form of care for oneself and others. From her, I learned that perseverance has value only when balanced with self-leadership. My mother's influence is evident in my refusal to conflate sacrifice with virtue.

My son has shaped me in ways no other relationship could. Being his mother has demanded honesty, growth, humility, and presence. He has challenged me to live the values I articulate and to choose transparency over comfort, boundaries over performance, and integrity over ease. Through my son, I have learned that leadership begins at home, that love does not require self-abandonment, and that self-respect is among the most enduring gifts a parent can give.

This book exists because of what my grandmother and my mother gave me, and what I continue to learn from my son.

This book is written with gratitude for the women who came before me and with responsibility to the generation watching what I choose next.

Introduction

Why Agility Matters More Than Ever

There is a subtle frustration among many women over 50—an emotion that does not always find expression but manifests as fatigue, disappointment, and resignation.

It manifests as a sense of chest tightness when a text message goes unanswered. As the mental calculus of whether to follow up or stay silent. As the exhaustion from doing everything right, yet still being told to wait, sets in.

At this stage of life, you have lived. You have loved and lost. You have built and rebuilt. You healed, achieved, sacrificed, and grew. You have learned the hard way. You know what peace feels like—and what chaos costs. You are no longer guessing your way through relationships; you are navigating them with awareness earned through experience.

And yet, here you are, moving through a dating landscape that feels more unstable than it did decades ago.

In the third decade of the twenty-first century—the mid-2020s—dating after 50 is not simply about finding companionship. It is about navigating emotional immaturity, avoidance of accountability, and men who seek access without responsibility—often while women are expected to remain patient, flexible, understanding, and even grateful for attention that leads nowhere. This creates a particular kind of dissonance.

Women come with clarity, while men come with conditions. Women have already done the work, whereas men are still figuring things out. Women look for partnership, but men seek options. This isn't due to a lack of interest; rather, it's a matter of misalignment.

This book exists because that narrative is no longer acceptable.

Agility Over 50 is not about teaching women

to compete for men, fix men, wait for men, or lower standards to accommodate men who refuse to grow. It is not a guide to endurance, patience, or emotional over-functioning.

"It's about movement".

"It's about discernment in action".

"It concerns inner strength — not control over others, but personal power".

Agility involves understanding when to engage, pause, pivot, or walk away without feeling guilty or needing to explain. It requires responding to the current reality rather than being influenced by fantasy, nostalgia, or social conditioning that encourages women to value harmony over honesty.

Many women over 50 are discovering an uncomfortable reality: the dating pool is not shallow because of women's age. It is shallow because too many men were never required to be partners.

This book does not shame men, but it does

not excuse dysfunction either. It delineates patterns that a significant subset of women have observed but seldom felt free to articulate: men who resist commitment for extended periods, pursue independence into later years, and seek stability only after a health crisis, a loneliness crisis, or a major life disruption—when the costs of independence ultimately become apparent.

Meanwhile, women are expected to be ready when that awakening arrives. Available. Forgiving. Accommodating. As if clarity must always yield to timing.

Agility Over 50 invites a different question: Is this partnership aligned with who I am now—or with who I was once taught to accommodate?

This book is about elevating awareness, shifting behavior, and renewing how you define love, partnership, and fulfillment—on your terms. It is about applying discernment where endurance was once expected, and self-leadership where self-sacrifice was once praised.

You're not late, behind, or overexerting yourself. We live in a time that calls for a new way of moving, where agility is essential.

CHAPTER 1

This Is Not Your Mother's Dating Pool

One of the most destabilizing realizations for women dating over 50 is not rejection—it is confusion.

Several women reach this stage emotionally prepared, clear about their worth, and open to partnership. They have lived long enough to understand what they want, and, more importantly, what they no longer want. They enter dating with grounded expectations rather than illusions.

Yet, what they face is not a lack of interest, but an absence of clarity: men who engage without intention, connect without commitment, and label their limitations without assuming responsibility for their impact.

Certain men go so far as to state plainly that they "have an issue with commitment," as if labeling the problem excuses them from any responsibility to address it. The disclosure is often framed as authenticity, vulnerability, or emotional self-awareness. In practice, it functions more like a disclaimer—an attempt to manage expectations while still benefiting from connection, intimacy, and companionship.

This is not an isolated experience.

It is a pattern.

Social scientists and clinicians have increasingly examined this dating pattern among people over 50. Exploration of adult connection, emotional development, and post-divorce behavior suggests that demonstrative maturity does not progress automatically with age. While a disproportionate number of women continue to refine relational skills through reflection and self-examination, a considerable number of men experience emotional development later—often prompted by disruption rather than intention.

Extended autonomy, shifting social norms, and reduced pressure to form or sustain long-term partnerships have altered the incentives for growth. The result is a dating landscape in which emotional readiness varies widely—not by age alone, but by willingness to engage in accountability.

Over time, I came to understand this pattern not intellectually but experientially.

I met accomplished, intelligent, socially functional, and outwardly self-sufficient men well into their fifties who were candid about their reluctance to commit. Some framed it as a personal flaw they were "working on," while others described it as a preference, a lifestyle choice, or a hard-earned independence.

What struck me was not their honesty but their comfort with remaining unchanged. They did not express urgency to evolve. They did not take accountability for how their avoidance affected others. They often expected women to accept this limitation while continuing to invest emotionally.

That expectation—quiet, unspoken, and normalized—became impossible to ignore.

It led me to a realization that sits at the foundation of this book:

Self-awareness without accountability is not maturity. It is stagnation.

In earlier generations, lack of commitment was often contextual. Career pressures, financial instability, family obligations, and social norms shaped relationship timelines. Commitment among both women and men was delayed but not dismissed.

In contrast, in the third decade of the twenty-first century, refusal to commit is frequently framed as emotional honesty rather than emotional avoidance—especially among men over 50. But naming the issue does not resolve it.

Recognizing a limitation does not necessarily indicate emotional maturity. Emotional maturity is shown by taking responsibility for the consequences of that limitation—both for oneself and for others.

A meaningful share of men over 50 have become fluent in the language of self-description without engaging in self-examination. They articulate their fears, preferences, and boundaries clearly, yet often resist change.

Disclosure becomes a substitute for growth. When this happens, the burden quietly shifts. Women are placed in a position where they must make decisions about:

- Whether to accept less than what they want.
- Whether to wait indefinitely.
- Whether to hope for evolution without evidence.
- Whether to compromise clarity in exchange for access.

This dynamic is not accidental.

It is systemic.

Women, particularly those over 50, have been socialized to be patient, flexible, and emotionally accommodating. Meanwhile, men are often socially permitted to remain emotionally noncommittal while still engaging in relationships that offer validation, comfort, and connection.

Emotional labor is not distributed equally, and accountability is often applied inconsistently.

Over time, it became clear that dating over 50 is not primarily about finding men. It is about navigating emotional immaturity that has been socially permitted to persist unchecked. Refusal to commit is rarely about fear alone. More often, it reflects:

- Avoidance of responsibility.
- Resistance to compromise.
- Discomfort with emotional accountability.
- A desire to retain control without obligation.

These patterns do not fade with age. More often than not, they become entrenched, reinforced by decades of social acceptance and personal rationalization.

Agility emerges when women stop interpreting non-commitment as temporary confusion and start recognizing it as data.

Men who say they cannot commit are often telling the truth. The mistake is to assume that awareness equals readiness or that patience will convert limitation into capacity.
This is not your mother's dating pool.

The cultural landscape has undergone a transformation. Men are no longer subject to the same pressures to develop emotionally as women. Emotional growth is now regarded as optional rather than required. Accountability is frequently postponed rather than mandated. Consequently, the dating environment requires active effort to establish clarity rather than presuming it.

For women over 50, agility means adjusting expectations—not downward, but accurately. It means understanding that emotional immaturity does not dissolve with time. It also means recognizing when potential is used as a placeholder for action.

It means refusing to organize one's life around someone else's limitations.
The goal of agility is not judgment.
It is discernment.

Agility empowers women to listen attentively, trust what is said, observe actions clearly, and respond accordingly—without resentment, justification, or self-betrayal.
That is the mindset needed now.
Not endurance.
Not hope.
Not performance.
Clarity.

CHAPTER 2

The Myth of "Plenty of Fish"

"Plenty of fish in the sea" is often offered as reassurance. In practice, it serves as a dismissal. It implies abundance where there is misalignment, choice where there is constraint, and opportunity where there is often emotional scarcity.

For women over 50 dating in the third decade of the twenty-first century, the phrase obscures the real issue: the challenge is not access to men but finding men capable of partnership.

This chapter aims to replace comfort with clarity.

Availability Is Not Capacity

One of the most persistent misunderstandings in modern dating is conflating availability with readiness.

A common pattern among men in the dating pool is that they are technically available. They are divorced, single, dating, and active on dating apps. However, availability is a logistical matter, not an emotional one. Capacity refers to the ability to:

- Sustain emotional connection over time.
- Navigate discomfort without withdrawing.
- Compromise without resentment.
- Take accountability when impact does not match intention.
- Integrate another person into a life structured around autonomy.

A man can be available yet still lack relational capacity. In fact, a notable portion of men over 50 remain in the dating pool precisely because they never felt compelled to leave it.

Here, agility requires distinguishing between presence and capacity.

The Illusion of Abundance in App-Based Dating

Dating apps simulate abundance while quietly undermining discernment. Endless profiles create the illusion of choice, yet the structure rewards:

- Low investment.
- Optional engagement.
- Replaceability.
- Emotional minimalism.

When alternatives feel infinite, accountability weakens. The ability to "keep looking" becomes a substitute for the discipline required to build something real. For men already resistant to commitment, app culture amplifies avoidance. For women seeking partnership, it creates confusion— because volume masquerades as opportunity.

Having abundance without discernment doesn't lead to power; instead, it results in noise.

Emotional Hoarding: Connection Without Commitment

A defining pattern in later-life dating is emotional hoarding. Emotional hoarding occurs when someone:

- Maintains multiple low-effort connections.
- Seeks validation without vulnerability.
- Engages in intimacy without progression.
- Keeps options open to avoid emotional risk.

This behavior is often rationalized as "keeping things light" or "not rushing." In practice, it allows emotional needs to be met without accountability. Women experience this as follows:

- Inconsistent communication.
- Periodic reappearances.
- Stalled momentum.
- Confusing mixed signals.

This is not emotional openness.

It is emotional containment.

12

Mismatched Timelines of Emotional Growth

One of the most destabilizing dynamics for women over 50 is asymmetry. A substantial share of women enter later-life dating after years of reflection, healing, and boundary-setting. A large share of men still arrive negotiating for autonomy—often for the first time. This creates a structural mismatch:

- Women seek integration.
- Men protect independence.

This is not a moral failure.

It is a developmental gap.

Agility requires recognizing the mismatch without assuming responsibility for closing it.

The Scarcity Narrative Placed on Women

Women over 50 are often told—explicitly and implicitly—to be realistic, flexible, and grateful. Scarcity is treated as fact:

- Time is running out.
- Options are limited.

- Compromise is required.

Scarcity is not neutral.

It functions as leverage.

When women believe in scarcity, standards soften, boundaries loosen, and discernment erodes. Relationships are accepted not because they are aligned but because they are available. Scarcity is not a fact.

It is a tactic.

Quality Is Not a Consolation Prize

A smaller dating pool does not diminish influence; rather, it concentrates on it. In leadership and systems design, having fewer options can lead to better outcomes. Exercising selectivity reduces waste, and exercising discernment increases efficiency. Agility reframes selectivity as strength.

You do not need many options.

You need aligned options.

Why Men Stay in the Pool Longer

Men often stay in the dating pool longer because the system allows it. They benefit from:

- Lower expectations for emotional labor.
- Social permission to delay commitment.
- Access to companionship without obligation.
- Minimal consequences for inconsistency.

The pool persists not because men are confused but because non-commitment is supported. Understanding this eliminates self-blame.

The Cost of Believing the Myth

Believing in "plenty of fish" has a real cost:

- Time invested in non-viable connections.
- Emotional energy spent decoding ambiguity.
- Peace sacrificed to uncertainty.
- Hope misallocated to potential.

Agility is cost-awareness.

Wise movement requires accurate data.

The Agile Woman's Lens

An agile woman does not interpret the dating pool emotionally. She interprets it strategically.

She asks:

1. What patterns am I seeing?
2. What behavior repeats?
3. What costs am I incurring?
4. What actually adds to my life?

She avoids arguing with reality. Instead, she responds to it. Agility isn't pessimism; it's about precision.

CHAPTER 3

When Accomplishment Becomes Intimidation

Once the myth of "plenty of fish" is dismantled, a deeper truth often emerges for women over 50: the challenge is not a lack of interest but resistance to equal-term partnerships.

A well-established pattern among women entering later-life dating is that they are accomplished and financially, emotionally, and professionally grounded. They have navigated careers, leadership roles, adversity, and reinvention. They are not seeking rescue. They are seeking reciprocity.

Yet this very stability can create friction. Not because accomplishment is threatening, but because it eliminates ambiguity.

Accomplishment Reveals, It Does Not Create Insecurity

As established in Chapter 2, availability does not equal capacity. That distinction becomes unmistakable when a woman's life is already stable.

An accomplished woman does not need validation to sustain a connection. She expects mutual effort, emotional literacy, and accountability. For men who have not developed these capacities, that clarity can feel destabilizing. Accomplishment does not create imbalance.
It exposes the imbalance.

When a woman does not need reassurance, rescue, or dependency, the relational dynamic shifts. There is nowhere to hide behind vagueness, charm, or delay. Expectations are clear, and patterns are easier to observe. Avoidance loses its cover.
This is often the moment discomfort appears.

Equality Feels Like Exposure to the Unprepared

A significant portion of men are comfortable with relationships characterized by asymmetric effort and diffuse responsibility. These dynamics enable connection without sustained accountability.

When a woman arrives grounded and self-defined, those dynamics are disrupted. What is sometimes labeled as intimidation is more accurately exposure.

An accomplished woman does not demand dominance. She demands definition.

She asks questions that demand answers. She notices patterns without dismissing them. She values presence over performance.

For men accustomed to relational flexibility without consequences, this shift can feel confrontational—even when it is calm.

When Achievement Triggers Deflection

This dynamic became especially evident in my experience after earning my Ph.D.

Instead of showing curiosity or engagement, some men made casual, unsolicited comments— comments that portrayed the achievement as a liability rather than as a source of respect. Phrases like "You have a Ph.D.; you should already know that" frequently appeared during disagreements or when setting boundaries.

These comments were not about intellectual exchange. They were about power.

The degree symbolized authority, earned expertise, and independence. For men already uneasy about equality, it disrupted familiar hierarchies. Instead of engaging as intellectual peers, some men deflected by invoking credentials to diminish rather than to understand.

What became clear was that insecurity often disguises itself as humor, sarcasm, or misplaced expectations. By invoking the achievement, responsibility subtly shifted from mutual engagement to justification for disengagement. The accomplishment did not cause discomfort. It revealed the discomfort.

The Mislabeling of Standards as "Too Much"

One of the most persistent narratives women face is the belief that their standards are extreme. Yet clarity is not excess.

Expecting consistency, accountability, emotional presence, and effort is not intimidation; it is the foundation of partnership. When these expectations are labeled as unreasonable, responsibility is quietly shifted back to women to soften, reassure, or self-edit. Agility requires refusing the transfer.

Standards are not demands.

They are filters.

Why Accomplishment Disrupts Avoidance

Avoidance thrives on ambiguity. Accomplished women bring clarity. They articulate their needs, set boundaries, and insist on reciprocity. This makes it difficult to:

- Drift indefinitely.
- Delay decisions without consequence.
- Maintain connection without contribution.

For men accustomed to emotional flexibility without accountability, this can feel restrictive—not because expectations are unfair, but because women demand engagement.

Agility means recognizing that resistance is not about incompatibility but about readiness.

Not All Discomfort Leads to Growth

Discomfort is often framed as evidence of growth, yet not all discomfort is developmental.

Growth-oriented discomfort fosters curiosity, reflection, and effort. Avoidance-driven discomfort fosters defensiveness, withdrawal, or subtle undermining.

An agile woman does not confuse discomfort with progress. She observes responses over time.

Words matter less than behavior.

Intentions matter less than patterns.

The Trap of Making Yourself Smaller

When an accomplishment is met with hesitation, a disproportionate number of women instinctively adjust their behavior.

They minimize success.

They lower expectations.

They over-explain.

This rarely creates safety.

It creates erosion.

Over time, women begin to disappear from relationships that cannot hold their full presence. Agility is the refusal to shrink in order to sustain connection.

You do not become more compatible by becoming less yourself.

Reframing Intimidation as Information

Intimidation is not a verdict.
It is data.

It reveals who is prepared for equality and who is not. An agile woman does not internalize intimidation; she recognizes it for what it is.

Compatibility is not chemistry alone.
It is shared readiness.

From Abundance Myths to Alignment Truths

Chapter 2 dismantled the illusion of abundance. This chapter sharpens the lens even further. The goal is not to find someone willing to tolerate your success. It is to find someone who can stand beside you without requiring you to step back.

Accomplishment is not an obstacle.

It is the filter.

Agility means trusting it.

CHAPTER 4

Men Who Want Freedom, Not Partnership

Freedom has become one of the most misunderstood concepts in modern dating.

It is often framed as self-knowledge, independence, or personal growth. In theory, these are healthy aims. In practice, however, freedom is often used as a buffer, shielding individuals from vulnerability, accountability, and sustained emotional responsibility.

This chapter examines freedom-seeking not as a moral failing, but as a relational pattern—one that has become increasingly visible in later-life dating.

Freedom as a Substitute for Readiness

A recurring pattern among men over 50 is to describe themselves as independent, self-sufficient, and uninterested in "complicating" their lives. On the surface, these qualities seem grounded and self-aware. Beneath them, however, lies a reluctance to integrate another person into a life already optimized for autonomy. Freedom becomes the justification for:

- Avoiding compromise.
- Resisting relational definition.
- Maintaining emotional distance.
- Opting out of difficult conversations.
- Preserving unilateral control.

The issue is not independence.

It is non-integration.

Partnership does not require the loss of self. It requires flexibility. When freedom is prioritized over mutuality, partnership is quietly disqualified.

Access Without Obligation

One of the most common expressions of freedom-seeking behavior is the desire for access without obligation. This often takes the form of:

- Companionship without consistency.
- Intimacy without progression.
- Emotional support without reciprocity.
- Presence without planning.

Freedom, in this context, allows individuals to enjoy emotional closeness without making a relational investment.

Agility requires recognizing when freedom is being used not as a value but as a shield.

Freedom-Seeking Is Not Gendered—But It Is Patterned

While this chapter focuses largely on men, it is important to be clear: freedom-seeking behavior is not exclusive to men. Some women also prioritize autonomy to the point that partnership becomes incompatible with their lifestyle. Others maintain emotional distance while remaining connected. Still others avoid commitment, framing disengagement as self-protection or as a form of independence.

Avoidance is not gendered.

Emotional unavailability is not gendered.
What differs is the interpretation of the behavior.

Men who resist commitment are often described as independent or noncommittal. Women who do the same are more likely to be labeled as guarded, closed, or emotionally unavailable. The behavior may be similar; the social narrative is not.

Agility requires recognizing freedom-seeking wherever it appears—and responding consistently.

Freedom Without Accountability Is Not Neutral

Freedom becomes problematic when it consistently benefits one person at the expense of another.

When someone repeatedly avoids:

- Clarifying intentions
- Adjusting their behavior
- Addressing emotional effects
- Sharing responsibility

It ceases to be a personal value and instead creates a relational imbalance.

Mutuality cannot exist where accountability is optional. An agile woman understands that partnership is not sustained by good intentions alone but by shared responsibility for the impact of choices on the relationship.

Why Freedom Appeals Later in Life

For many people over 50, freedom is framed as earned. After years of marriage, caregiving, professional obligations, or sacrifice, autonomy can feel like a form of restoration.

Wanting space, control, and self-direction is natural. What becomes problematic is when freedom is protected at all costs—even when a desire for connection persists. Wanting autonomy and wanting partnership are not mutually exclusive. Refusing to reconcile them is a choice.

Agility means respecting that choice without trying to negotiate against it.

Freedom vs. Partnership: A Necessary Distinction

Freedom prioritizes individual preferences.
Partnership prioritizes shared consideration.
Freedom protects control.
Partnership requires collaboration.

Neither is inherently wrong, but they are not interchangeable.
Clarity—not persuasion—is the solution.

An agile woman does not try to convert freedom into readiness. She recognizes readiness when it arises.

The Emotional Cost to Women

Freedom-seeking dynamics often place the emotional labor on women. Women are expected to:

- Be flexible around schedules.
- Accept ambiguity without complaint.
- Tolerate inconsistency.
- Regulate disappointment quietly.

Over time, this creates erosion—not because women lack resilience, but because imbalance accumulates.

Agility restores balance by refusing to normalize one-sided adaptation.

The Agile Response

Agility does not argue with freedom-seeking behavior.

It responds.

An agile woman:

- Listen carefully to how freedom is described.

- Observes whether actions align with stated intentions.
- Assesses whether compromise is possible—or resisted.
- Chooses alignment over potential.

She does not take freedom personally.

She does not internalize it as rejection.

She recognizes it as information.

Choosing Alignment Over Attachment

Freedom-seeking individuals are not villains.

They simply do not align with partnership.

Agility means allowing people to be who they are—without reorganizing your life around who they are not.

This is not rejection.

It is discernment.

When practiced consistently, discernment is a form of self-respect.

CHAPTER 5

The Health-Crisis Commitment Phenomenon

There is a pattern many women over 50 recognize instinctively, even if they hesitate to name it.

A man avoids commitment for years. He values autonomy, flexibility, and independence. He resists integration, postpones time together, and attributes the distance to busyness, timing, or personal preference.

Then a health crisis occurs.

A heart attack.

A stroke.

A sudden confrontation with mortality.

Almost overnight, the man who guarded his freedom seeks closeness, connection, and consistency.

This chapter examines that shift—not with judgment, but with clarity.

Crisis Does Not Create Readiness—It Reveals Need

Health crises do not magically confer emotional maturity; rather, they reveal vulnerability.

In moments of physical decline, fear intensifies. Independence grows fragile. The cost of isolation becomes clear. What once felt like freedom now feels like risk. The desire for partnership emerges—but not always from growth.

Agility requires distinguishing between need-based attachment and readiness-based partnership.

One seeks relief.

The other offers reciprocity.

This distinction matters because urgency can mimic intimacy, and vulnerability can feel like openness. However, emotional exposure—without responsibility or capacity—does not automatically translate into partnership.

Agility creates the pause needed to distinguish between need and readiness.

Why Health Events Trigger Sudden Attachment

Later-life health events disrupt long-standing illusions of control. They force individuals to confront:

- Dependency.
- Aging.
- Mortality.
- Loneliness.
- The limits of autonomy.

For men who have characterized themselves by independence, this disruption can be profound. Self-sufficiency, once a source of pride, is now uncertain. Familiar routines are disrupted. Physical resilience is no longer assured.

Sudden outreach, increased communication, and urgent bids for connection are often less about love and more about stability, reassurance, and care.

This is not inherently wrong, but it does require discernment.

Agility does not dismiss vulnerability.
It refuses to conflate vulnerability with readiness.

Avoidance Before the Crisis Matters

One of the most overlooked aspects of this pattern is the period preceding the health event.

Agility looks both backwards and forward. Men who seek closeness after a crisis often have:

- Repeated opportunities for connection.
- Invitations to spend time together.
- Chances to build a relational foundation.

Their absence was not accidental.

It was intentional.

Crisis does not erase that history.

It contextualizes it.

A health event may explain a sudden shift, but it does not retroactively transform years of avoidance into evidence of partnership capacity. Agility holds both timelines simultaneously.

A Common Observation

It is not uncommon for women to notice the following pattern:

- A man over 50 consistently declines.
- Opportunities to deepen connection.
- Time together is postponed.
- Engagement is minimal.
- Availability is conditional.
- Excuses are frequent.

Then a serious health event occurs—a heart attack, a stroke, or a loss of physical or cognitive function. Suddenly, communication intensifies. Calls become more frequent. The desire for closeness deepens.

What has changed is not emotional capacity. What has changed is the need.

In these moments, partnership is often sought not as a mutual exchange but as a support system.

Agility requires asking a difficult but necessary question: Is this a request for a relationship or for care? The answer determines everything that follows.

The Unspoken Expectation of Female Caretaking

Health crises often activate deeply ingrained gender norms.

Women are socialized to nurture, manage, and sacrifice. Men—particularly those accustomed to independence—may unconsciously expect emotional and physical caregiving without renegotiating the relationship. The assumption is subtle but powerful:

- That availability will increase.
- That sacrifice will be offered.

- That care will be provided without discussion.

Agility disrupts this assumption.

Care is not owed because of vulnerability.

Care is negotiated through mutual commitment.

Without that negotiation, women are often assigned roles they did not consent to.

Need Is Not the Same as Partnership

There is a critical distinction between:

- Wanting someone because you are afraid.
- Wanting someone because you are aligned.

Fear-driven attachments often convey urgency.

A growth-driven partnership necessitates responsibility.

Urgency accelerates access.

Responsibility sustains connection.

Agility enables compassion without obligation.

You can acknowledge vulnerability without internalizing it.

You can care without committing.

You can listen without reorganizing your life.

This is not a withdrawal.

It is discernment.

Why Women Feel Torn in These Moments

Women frequently encounter profound internal conflict when confronted with attachment driven by crisis. Women feel:

- Empathy for the health event.
- Guilt for hesitating.
- Pressure to show up.
- Confusion about boundaries.

This conflict is not a weakness.

It is conditioning.

Agility means honoring compassion without overriding discernment. It allows women to care without surrendering their agency. You are not required to solve what someone else deferred.

The Cost of Confusing Crisis with Commitment

When a crisis is mistaken for readiness, women often find themselves:

- Providing care without reciprocity.
- Sacrificing time, energy, or stability.
- Entering unequal dynamics.
- Becoming essential without being chosen.

This is not a partnership.

It is caretaking without consent.

Over time, these arrangements quietly erode peace, dignity, and self-trust.

Agility protects against that erosion by asking better questions sooner.

The Agile Response

An agile woman pauses.

She asks:

- What was available before the crisis?
- What is being asked of me now?
- What would this require me to sacrifice?

- Is there mutuality—or urgency?

She does not rush to fill gaps created by someone else's avoidance.

Agility does not deny vulnerability.

It refuses to be recruited into imbalance.

Compassion Without Self-Erasure

You are allowed to care.

You are allowed to say no.

You are allowed to set boundaries while dealing with illness.

Health events do not entitle anyone to access that they previously declined to build.

Agility honors humanity and self-respect.

From Crisis to Clarity

This chapter is not about rejecting men in times of need.

It is about choosing a partnership rooted in intention—not in an emergency.

Late-life connections should be built on shared readiness, not on fear of decline.

Agility means understanding the difference and acting accordingly.

CHAPTER 6

Stop Dating for Potential

If there is one habit that consistently undermines women over 50 in dating, it is not optimism—it is projection.

Dating for potential is the practice of engaging with who someone could become rather than who they consistently demonstrate. It is fueled by hope, reinforced by patience, and sustained by empathy. It is also one of the costliest patterns women carry into later-life relationships.

This chapter is not meant to discourage hope. It is about nurturing it.

Potential Is Not a Relationship

Potential is an idea; a relationship is a practice. Potential exists in the future, while relationships take place in the present.

When women date for potential, they often substitute intention for action and interpretation for evidence. This substitution creates an imbalance:

- Effort is extended without return.
- Time is invested without a trajectory.
- Emotional labor increases as clarity decreases.

Potential invites imagination.

Relationships require participation.

Agility begins when women stop mistaking possibility for probability.

Why Potential Feels So Persuasive

Potential is compelling because it speaks directly to a woman's strengths.

Women over 50 are often emotionally perceptive, development-oriented, and skilled at fostering growth. These qualities serve them well in leadership, family, and community settings.

In dating, however, they can quietly become liabilities when reciprocity is absent.

Seeing the possibility is not the problem. Staying when reality contradicts it is.

Potential feels generous.

It feels patient.

It feels humane.

However, generosity without limits can lead to depletion.

Patience without progress becomes stagnation.

Agility does not punish hope.

It disciplines it.

Potential Thrives Where Accountability Is Absent

Men who are unclear, inconsistent, or avoidant often benefit from being seen as "almost ready." Language becomes a substitute for action:

- "I'm working on myself."
- "I just need time."
- "I'm not there yet."

- "I've never felt this way before."

Without follow-through, these statements function merely as placeholders—sustaining emotional engagement without necessitating behavioral change.

Accountability turns intention into action. Without it, potential becomes a holding pattern.

Agility requires measuring commitment by pattern, not by promise.

Necessary Recalibration

Many women, including me, reach a point when optimism needs recalibration.

Not abandoned—but grounded.

This shift is not from hope to hardness but from projection to precision. It is the moment when emotional intelligence is no longer used to explain away inconsistency but to recognize it.

Recalibration is not pessimism.

It is maturity.

Agility begins when women stop using their insight to rescue potential and start using it to assess reality.

Age Does Not Reduce the Cost of Waiting

Waiting does not get easier with age.
It becomes more expensive. At this stage of life:

- Time carries greater value.
- Energy is more finite.
- Peace is harder won.
- Recovery from disappointment takes longer.

Dating for potential delays clarity—not because growth is impossible, but because growth cannot be outsourced to patience.

No amount of understanding can compensate for a lack of readiness.

Agility treats time as a finite resource.

The Emotional Labor Gap

Dating for potential often results in women taking on a disproportionate share of emotional labor. Women:

- Interpret ambiguity.
- Manage disappointment.
- Hold space for uncertainty.
- Keep hope alive for both parties.

This labor is rarely returned.

Over time, women begin shouldering the emotional weight of the relationship alone—tracking progress, managing expectations, and quietly absorbing disappointment.

Agility means refusing to carry emotional labor that is not shared equally.

Consistency Is the Only Credible Signal

Consistency matters more than chemistry.
Chemistry can be instantaneous.
Consistency is maintained.

Consistency reveals:

- Capacity.
- Values.
- Emotional regulation.
- Willingness to integrate another person into daily life.

Attraction may open the door.

Consistency determines who can walk through it.

Agility treats consistency as non-negotiable data.

When Potential Becomes Self-Betrayal

Believing in potential becomes self-abandonment when:

- Red flags are reframed as challenges.
- Boundaries are softened to preserve connection.
- Needs are postponed indefinitely.

At this point, hope no longer serves growth. It protects against avoidance.

Agility restores self-trust by honoring what is observable rather than imagined.

The Agile Reframe

An agile woman does not ask,

"Who could he become?"

She asks,

"Who is he choosing to be—consistently?"

Growth is welcome.

Avoidance is not.

This question shifts power back to discernment.

Stop Investing Ahead of Evidence

In leadership and systems thinking, investment follows proof of concept. The same holds true for dating.

When emotional investment precedes evidence, imbalance ensues.

When investment aligns with demonstrated effort, clarity follows.

Agility means aligning emotional investment with observable behavior—not with narrative, hope, or future projections.

Choosing Reality Over Narrative

Dating for potential often involves constructing explanations that mitigate misalignment.

Narratives provide comfort.

Reality provides direction.

Agility replaces narrative with data.

Reality is not cruel.

It is clarifying.

Reflection Questions (Chapter 6)

1. Where am I investing in potential rather than behavior?
1. What patterns am I repeatedly explaining instead of evaluating?
2. What would clarity require me to stop hoping for?
3. If nothing changed, would this still feel viable?
4. What does consistency look like for me now—in practice, not theory?

CHAPTER 7

Emotional Agility Over Emotional Availability

Emotional availability is often treated as a universal virtue in dating. Women are encouraged to be open, expressive, and receptive—sometimes without equal emphasis on discernment, pacing, or boundaries.

Emotional agility reframes this expectation.

Agility does not suppress emotion.

It is about deploying emotion intentionally.

This distinction is subtle—but it changes everything.

Availability Is Not a Strategy

In leadership systems, availability without prioritization leads to burnout. Leaders who respond equally to requests, issues, and stakeholders create fragility rather than resilience. Dating follows the same principle.

Emotional availability without structure invites overextension. It signals accessibility without accountability and openness without pacing. Over time, it blurs expectations and shifts responsibility to the most emotionally available person present.

Agility means deciding when, how, and to whom emotional access is granted.

Availability alone does not create a connection. Intentional engagement does.

Emotional Agility as Adaptive Capacity

In organizational systems, agility means responding to change without disrupting core operations. Similarly, emotionally agile women act in this way. Women who are emotionally agile:

- Stay open without being porous.
- Engage without over-investing.
- Respond without absorbing.

- Adjust without abandoning themselves.

This is not detachment.

It is adaptive capacity.

Emotional agility allows women to remain responsive to connection without losing coherence. It preserves internal stability amid external dynamics.

Boundaries as System Architecture

Boundaries are frequently perceived as walls. In systems design, boundaries serve an architectural purpose—they define interactions between components and ensure the system's functionality. Without boundaries:

- Systems overload.
- Signals get distorted.
- Resources are depleted.
- Failures cascade.

Emotional boundaries serve the same purpose. They protect clarity, conserve energy, and preserve integrity.

Boundaries are not barriers to intimacy. They are the conditions that sustain intimacy over time. Agility recognizes that intimacy without structure collapses under pressure.

Why Over-Availability Creates Instability

Effective leadership is characterized by teams functioning optimally when expectations are clearly communicated and roles are clearly delineated. Ambiguity leads to confusion and reduced efficiency.

In the context of dating, over-availability introduces ambiguity by:

- Removing pacing.
- Obscuring roles.
- Eliminating feedback loops.

When emotional access is immediate and unlimited, there is little incentive for intentional engagement. Effort becomes optional, and reciprocity becomes unclear. The relationship loses structure before it has a foundation.

Agility introduces containment—not restriction, but coherence.

Signal vs. Noise in Emotional Communication

High-performing systems distinguish signal from noise, prioritizing meaningful data and filtering out distractions. Emotionally agile women do the same. They notice:

- Who responds consistently.
- Who follows through.
- Who adjusts behaviors.
- Who engages under pressure.

They do not overreact to intensity or overlook inconsistencies. They do not confuse emotional stimulation with emotional reliability.

Agility values signal over-stimulation.

Emotional Availability Without Reciprocity Is Technical Debt

In technology, technical debt accumulates when short-term solutions are prioritized over sustainable design. Although systems may work initially, instability compounds over time, making failure inevitable.

In dating, emotional over-availability creates relational debt and an imbalance:

- One person regulates emotions.
- One person carries uncertainty.
- One person invests ahead of evidence.

The cost is not immediate.

It accumulates quietly.

Agility addresses imbalance early—before debt compounds and collapse becomes inevitable.

The Role of Pacing

In agile systems, pacing prevents overload and enables iteration. Dating benefits from the same discipline. Pacing allows:

- Observation.
- Adjustment.
- Trust-building.
- Informed decision-making.

Urgency undermines learning.

Pacing preserves clarity.

Agility resists acceleration not because the connection is unwelcome but because sustainability outweighs speed.

Emotional Agility in Practice

Emotionally agile women:

- Match energy, not exceed it.
- Respond rather than react.
- Clarify rather than assume.
- Exit rather than endure.

They do not confuse availability with worth.

They do not equate effort with value.

They allow behavior to reveal capacity.

Agility replaces over-functioning with observation.

Resilience Over Exposure

Resilient systems remain adaptable under pressure because of their careful design. Emotional resilience is built through:

- Self-regulation.
- Clear standards.
- Feedback awareness.
- Strategic openness.

Vulnerability without regulation leads to volatility.

Agility allows vulnerability without volatility.

This is not emotional withdrawal.

It is emotional stewardship.

The Agile Reframe

Emotional availability is openness.

Emotional agility is governance.

One invites connection.

The other sustains it.

Agility is the discipline that allows openness to endure without self-erosion.

Reflection Questions (Chapter 7)

1. Where am I emotionally over-available without reciprocity?

2. What boundaries would increase—not limit—connection?
3. How do I distinguish consistency from intensity?
4. Where might pacing serve me better than urgency?
5. What does emotional agility look like for me in practice?

CHAPTER 8

Compromise vs. Self-Abandonment

Compromise is often described as the cornerstone of successful relationships. Women are taught that flexibility, accommodation, and understanding are signs of emotional maturity.

But not all compromise is mutual.

At this stage of life, one of the most critical distinctions women must learn to make is between compromise that strengthens connection and self-abandonment that erodes it.

This chapter is about drawing that line clearly—and holding it.

What Compromise Actually Is

In healthy systems— such as organizations, teams, or partnerships—compromise is a mutual process. It includes:

- Mutual adjustment.
- Shared inconvenience.
- Collective problem-solving.
- Respect for the impact on both parties.

Compromise assumes two people working toward alignment. It does not require one person to consistently absorb discomfort so the other can remain unchanged.

Healthy compromise distributes costs.

Self-abandonment concentrates them.

Agility requires knowing the difference.

What Self-Abandonment Looks Like

Self-abandonment often masquerades as maturity. It sounds like this:

- "It's not ideal, but I can live with it."
- "No one is perfect."

- "At least I won't be alone."
- "This is probably the best I can do at this age."

Over time, these justifications normalize imbalance. Self-abandonment occurs when:

- Your needs are postponed indefinitely.
- Your boundaries are softened to preserve access.
- Your discomfort is reframed as personal growth.
- Your expectations are treated as negotiable, but theirs are not.

This is not a compromise. It is a quiet erosion of identity, clarity, and self-trust.

Agility makes erosion visible before it becomes permanent.

Why Compromise Becomes More Dangerous Over 50

Earlier in life, compromise is often tied to building careers, families, and shared futures. Later in life, the context for compromise shifts.

You are no longer building from scratch.

You are integrating into an already full life.

The cost of compromise increases because:

- Time is more finite.
- Peace is harder earned.
- Capacity for recovery is reduced.
- You recognize misalignment more quickly.

What once felt tolerable now seems expensive.

Agility demands more precision, not less.

A Common Internal Negotiation

Many women over the age of 50 grapple with an unsettling internal dialogue:

- Perhaps I do not require everything.
- Perhaps companionship alone suffices.

- Perhaps this is simply their current reality.

There have been times when the idea of companionship, someone to converse with, share meals, and simply be with, tempted me to reevaluate the standards I have diligently upheld. This wasn't because those standards were lacking; rather, it came from realizing that loneliness can make compromise a sensible option.

Over time, I realized that compromising my needs to maintain companionship would have led me to diminish myself in unsustainable ways.

That realization was not dramatic.

It was clarifying.

Companionship gained through self-abandonment is not neutral. It quietly reshapes your relationship with yourself.

Agility honors that truth without shame.

The False Binary: Alone or Compromised

One of the most damaging narratives women face is the belief that the only alternatives are:

- Being alone.
- Being partnered at a cost.

This is a false binary.

Agility introduces a third option: alignment—or nothing.

Being alone doesn't necessarily lead to feelings of unfulfillment, and being in a relationship doesn't automatically mean you'll receive support.

A relationship that requires you to disappear is not a solution to loneliness; it is a relocation of loneliness.

How Self-Abandonment Gets Rationalized

Self-abandonment rarely arrives all at once. It enters quietly through small concessions:

- Accepting inconsistent communication.
- Overlooking dismissive comments.

- Reducing expectations for effort.
- Tolerating emotional distance.

Each concession feels manageable.

The accumulation does not.

Over time, women begin to adapt rather than to assess.

Agility requires monitoring patterns, not moments.

Compromise That Is Worth Making

A healthy compromise remains possible—and worth pursuing. It encompasses:

- Modifying preferences, not core values.
- Sharing inconvenience, rather than absorbing it entirely.
- Negotiating logistics arrangements, without compromising dignity.
- Adjusting habits, without infringing upon boundaries.

The test is simple:

- Does this compromise make the relationship stronger—or just quieter?

Quiet is not alignment.

Silence is not peace.

Agility protects the difference.

Why Women Are Socialized to Over-Compromise

Women are frequently complimented for their adaptability. Flexibility is often rewarded, endurance becomes common, and silence is mistaken for grace.

This conditioning is subtle yet powerful.

Agility challenges it.

At this stage of life, resilience does not mean tolerating more. It means demanding better.

The Agile Reframe

An agile woman does not ask:

"Can I live with this?"

She asks,

"Does this allow me to remain fully myself?"

Compromising one's identity is too expensive.

Agility treats self-presence as non-negotiable.

Reflection Questions (Chapter 8)

1. Where have I compromised in ways that made me feel smaller?
2. What needs have I labeled "optional" to preserve companionship?
3. How do I typically justify staying in situations that feel misaligned?
4. What does sustainable companionship look like for me now?
5. Where is the line between flexibility and self-erasure in my life?

The Cost of Entertaining Unfinished Men

When engaging with unfinished men, not all expenses are immediately noticeable. Certain costs build up silently—by waiting, explaining, checking in, and hoping. Over time, these costs influence how women direct their energy, attention, and emotional effort.

This chapter is not about blame.

It is about cost awareness.

Agility is cost awareness: recognizing what something costs, not just how it feels.

Who Unfinished Men Are

An unfinished man is not defined by age, income, or intelligence. He is defined by relational incompleteness. He may be:

- Emotionally inconsistent.
- Unclear about intention.
- Resistant to accountability.
- Comfortable receiving without reciprocating.
- Dismissive of emotional impact.

He is not necessarily unkind. He is not necessarily malicious. He is simply unwilling—or unable—to enter into a partnership with that intent.

Agility requires recognizing this distinction early, before investment becomes entanglement.

How Investment Becomes One-Sided

One of the most prevalent patterns women experience is emotional asymmetry.

She:

- Thinks about him.
- Notices his absence.
- Tracks communication gaps.
- Feels responsible for maintaining contact.
- Interprets silence as a problem to manage.

Men generally tend to:

- Respond when convenient.
- Avoid follow-up.
- Leave messages unanswered.
- Assume availability without effort.

This imbalance rarely announces itself. It develops gradually—through accommodation, explanation, and quiet adjustment. Over time, emotional effort shifts from mutual engagement to unilateral maintenance.

Agility recognizes asymmetry before it is normalized.

A Common Observation

It is not uncommon for women to become emotionally invested in men who do not reciprocate. The pattern often unfolds like this:

- He is dismissive about returning calls.
- He initiates inconsistently.
- He does not follow through.
- He allows distance to persist.

Over time, the woman begins to feel responsible for the connection. She checks in when she hasn't heard from him, wondering if something is wrong. She feels obligated to maintain contact—despite receiving little evidence of his interest.

This obligation is not love.

It is conditioning.

Agility requires noticing the moment when concern supplants reciprocity.

The Emotional Labor Trap

Emotional labor often creeps in quietly.

It sounds like:

- "I don't want to seem uncaring."
- "He has a lot going on."
- "Maybe I should just check in."

What is rarely acknowledged is the following:

- Anxiety increases.
- Self-trust erodes.
- Power dynamics shift.
- Desire becomes pursuit.

Emotional labor transforms attraction into responsibility and curiosity into vigilance.

Agility interrupts this pattern early—before effort becomes an expectation.

Interest Does Not Require Chasing

My grandmother once said something simple that has consistently been proven accurate:

"If a man is interested in you, you will never have to chase him. He will go after what he wants—and make it clear."

This is not about ego.

It is about behavior.

Interest shows itself in effort.

Clarity shows itself in consistency.

When a pursuit becomes one-sided, the answer is not more effort—it is information.

Agility trusts that information.

Why Women Stay Engaged Anyway

Women often remain engaged because:

- They value connection.
- They are empathetic.
- They are patient.
- They want to believe effort will be met.

76

These qualities are strengths, but when applied without discernment, they become liabilities.

Empathy without boundaries becomes self-neglect.

Patience without evidence becomes delay.

Agility means applying empathy without obligation.

The Hidden Costs of Entertaining Unfinished Men

Dealing with unfinished men is more costly than just time; it incurs additional costs such as:

- Peace of mind.
- Emotional bandwidth.
- Self-respect.
- Opportunity for aligned connection.
- Trust in one's own instincts.

These costs compound quietly. What begins as flexibility becomes depletion. What begins as patience turns into self-doubt.

Agility recognizes when a connection is draining rather than developing it.

Silence Is Also Communication

One of the most challenging realities is that silence is never neutral. Delayed replies, unacknowledged calls, and unclear engagement all indicate how much something is—or isn't—a priority.

Silence does not require interpretation.

It requires acknowledgment.

Agility treats silence as information, not as a puzzle to be solved.

The Agile Response

An agile woman does not chase clarity.

She observes it.

She does not fill the gaps left by someone else's disengagement.

She allows space for truth to reveal itself—

because truth does not require pursuit.

Interest that must be pursued is unstable.

A connection that must be maintained alone is not a partnership.

Agility allows patterns to speak for themselves.

Choosing Self-Respect Over Access

Letting go of unfinished men is not a rejection.

It is reclamation.

It is reclaiming energy, attention, and dignity.

It is choosing alignment over proximity and self-respect over access.

Agility means no longer confusing attention with intention.

Reflection Questions (Chapter 9)

1. Where am I investing more emotional energy than I am receiving?

2. How do I respond when communication is inconsistent?

3. Have I mistaken concern or obligation for connection?

4. What behaviors signal genuine interest to me, and are they present?

5. What would change if I stopped filling in the gaps?

CHAPTER 10

Red Flags Don't Turn Green with Age

Experience does not erase patterns—it intensifies them. One of the most persistent misconceptions in later-life dating is that time, age, or circumstances will soften long-standing behavior. In reality, habits reinforced over decades become more entrenched, not more flexible.

This chapter is not about cynicism.

It is about accuracy.

Agility requires seeing what is, not what feels more comfortable to hope for.

Patterns Are Predictive

In every functioning system—organizational, relational, or social—past behavior is the most reliable predictor of future performance. When patterns repeat, they are not accidents.

This is data.

Inconsistent communication, avoidance of accountability, emotional withdrawal, and resistance to compromise are not transitional phases at this stage of life. They are established modes of operation.

Patterns persist because they work—for the person repeating them.

Agility requires trusting patterns over explanations, consistency over apologies, and behavior over narratives.

Age Adds Complexity, Not Correction

Age brings experience, not automatic evolution. Without intentional self-examination, growth does not occur by default.

In many cases, aging reinforces comfort with familiar behavior—especially when that behavior has been socially tolerated, rewarded, or accommodated. Red flags that appear earlier in life often evolve into:

- More refined.
- Better rationalized.
- More confidently defended.

The packaging changes.

The pattern does not.

Agility recognizes that time alone does not equal transformation.

The Myth of the "Late Bloomer"

The idea of the late bloomer is appealing. It suggests that growth is inevitable and that patience will ultimately be rewarded.

While growth is always possible, it is rarely accidental. Meaningful change requires:

- Self-awareness paired with accountability.
- Consistent effort over time.
- Willingness to experience discomfort.

- Observable behavior change—not intention statements.

Without these elements, waiting for transformation is self-deception.

Agility distinguishes between the capacity for growth and the evidence of it.

Why Red Flags Are Reinterpreted

Red flags are often reinterpreted because:

- Chemistry creates bias.
- Loneliness creates tolerance.
- Empathy creates justification.
- Hope creates narrative.

These forces are human.

They are also distorting.

As emotional investment increases, perception narrows. Women begin explaining behavior rather than evaluating it, thereby normalizing what once felt misaligned.

Agility means allowing clarity to take precedence over comfort.

84

Common Red Flags That Do Not Age Out

Certain behaviors reliably predict relational difficulties across ages and are considered to be:

- Chronic inconsistency.
- Defensiveness when confronted.
- Dismissal of emotional impact.
- Resistance to accountability.
- Blame-shifting.
- Avoidance of future-oriented conversations.

These are not quirks.

They are structural limitations.

Agility treats recurring patterns as constraints—not as challenges to overcome.

Impact Matters More Than Intention

A common defense for problematic behavior is the assertion of good intentions.

Intent does not negate impact.

In mature partnerships, responsibility means recognizing how actions affect others and adjusting accordingly.

When impact is consistently dismissed, emotional safety erodes—even when harm is unintentional.

Agility prioritizes outcomes over explanations.

Repair requires ownership.

Growth requires adjustment.

Without both, patterns persist.

Waiting Is Not a Strategy

Hope is not a plan.

Remaining in a dynamic characterized by red flags is often justified as follows:

- Time invested.
- Emotional attachment.
- Fear of starting over.
- Belief in eventual change.

None of these alters behavior.

Endurance is not evidence of progress.

Tolerance is not proof of maturity.

Agility recognizes that staying does not make something work.

Clarity Is an Act of Self-Respect

Acknowledging early red flags is not pessimistic.

It is self-respect.

Clarity protects:

- Time.
- Energy.
- Emotional health.
- Future possibility.

Ignoring red flags does not preserve a connection. It only delays disappointment.

Agility chooses truth early rather than recovery later.

The Agile Reframe

An agile woman does not ask:

"Can this improve?"

She asks,

"Is this already aligned?"

Alignment is not perfection.

It is compatible at the behavioral level.

Agility prioritizes livability—not a theoretical possibility. From Awareness to Action.

Red flags do not require debate.

They require a response.

Agility means acting on what you see—without apology, justification, or delay.

Growth may be possible.

But a partnership should not be built on probability alone.

Clarity is not harsh.

It is efficient.

CHAPTER 11

Choosing Peace Over Performance

Performance is one of the most invisible habits women bring into relationships. It does not announce itself as insecurity. Instead, it shows up as effort, patience, flexibility, and emotional generosity. It often looks like maturity. Over time, however, performance quietly replaces authenticity—peace becomes collateral damage.

This chapter is about recognizing when effort becomes self-monitoring and when connection becomes work.

What Performance Looks Like in Dating

Performance isn't about pretending to be someone else; it's about continuously adjusting who you are to stay connected. It manifests as:

- Overthinking responses.
- Monitoring tone and timing.
- Managing emotional temperature.
- Avoiding "too much" honesty.
- Carrying responsibility for relational comfort.

Performance is subtle.

And it is exhausting.

It does not feel dramatic. It feels responsible and considerate, and like staying ahead of discomfort so nothing breaks.

Why Women Perform

Women are often rewarded for relational fluency. They are taught to:

- Anticipate needs.
- Smooth tension.

- Regulate emotion.
- Preserve harmony.

In leadership systems, this invisible labor is recognized as emotional overhead. In dating, it is often mistaken for compatibility.

Agility requires naming the difference.

Compatibility reduces labor.

Performance increases labor.

How Performance Gets Reinforced

Performance rarely begins with self-erasure; it begins with success.

Early in a relationship, performance is often rewarded. Women are praised for being "easy to talk to," "low maintenance," "so understanding," or "emotionally intelligent." The ability to adapt, absorb, and accommodate fosters closeness quickly. It smooths over friction and keeps things moving.

Over time, however, what was once appreciated becomes expected. Flexibility is no longer noticed—it is assumed. Emotional regulation is no longer thanked for—it is relied on. The effort is no longer reciprocal—it is absorbed.

Performance becomes the price of admission. When a woman stops performing—pausing, speaking plainly, or withdrawing effort—the shift is immediate. Tension rises. Discomfort surfaces. The relationship reveals that acceptance was conditional on adjustment.

This is often the moment clarity arrives—not because something went wrong, but because something stopped being managed.

Peace Does Not Require Management.

Peace is not something you earn through effort.

In stable systems, peace is the result of alignment—not constant adjustment. When a relationship requires constant calibration to avoid discomfort, it is not peaceful. It is fragile.

Agility means noticing how much effort it takes to remain "okay."

Peace does not require vigilance.

Peace does not punish stillness.

Peace does not collapse when you stop managing it.

What Peace Actually Sounds Like in Real Time

Peace is frequently mistaken for silence or a lack of conflict. However, in truth, peace has its own unique quality. It can be described as:

- Pauses that are not punished.
- Silence that is not interrogated.
- Questions that do not trigger defensiveness.
- Needs that are not framed as an inconvenience.
- Differences that do not threaten the connection.

Peace does not require rehearsal.

Peace does not demand recovery after honesty.

Peace allows misunderstanding without withdrawal.

Peace is not perfection.

It is safe.

A Quiet Recognition

Many women reach a moment of quiet recognition—not after conflict, but after a calm.

It is the realization that even when nothing is wrong, something still feels like an effort. That connection requires vigilance. That ease never quite arrives.

This recognition is not dramatic.

It is decisive.

Agility begins when women trust that signal.

The Cost of Performing

Performance entails a greater expenditure than energy alone. It requires:

- Authentic expression.
- Emotional safety.
- Self-trust.
- Spontaneity.
- Joy.

Over time, women begin to disappear from relationships that demand constant self-adjustment. They become fluent and capable, yet quietly diminished.

Agility prevents that erosion.

Peace Is a Compatibility Metric

Peace is not passive.

It is diagnostic.

A relationship that allows you to:

- Speak freely.
- Be misunderstood without punishment.
- Express needs without fear.
- Exist without explanation.

is not rare—it is aligned.

Agility elevates peace from a preference to a requirement.

Why Performance Is Often Mistaken for Love

The sensation of productivity is apparent in performance. Effort may generate the illusion of engagement. Struggle can be mistaken for wisdom. Endurance may be mistaken for dedication.

But love that demands constant performance is unsustainable.

Agility reframes love as both ease and integrity.

The Agile Reframe

An agile woman does not ask:

"How do I keep this going?"

She asks,

"How does this feel to live inside?"

Peace is not the absence of conflict.

It is the absence of self-erasure.

Letting Ease Be the Standard

Choosing peace is not giving up love.

It is protecting well-being as a boundary, not a bargaining tool.

Agility means letting ease—not effort—be the measure of compatibility.

Transition: When Peace Becomes the Standard

When peace becomes non-negotiable, something profound shifts.

Performance loses its utility.

Endurance loses its status.

Partnership loses its urgency.

What remains is choice.

The next chapter explores what happens when partnership is no longer required to validate a life, but instead is invited to enhance it.

Reflection Questions (Chapter 11)

1. Where do I monitor myself to preserve connection?
2. What parts of me feel effortful to maintain in relationships?
3. When do I feel most at ease—and with whom?
4. How do I distinguish effort from alignment?

CHAPTER 12

Partnership Is an Option, Not a Requirement

For many women, partnership has been regarded as the paramount measure of fulfillment. It is marked by a sense of completion, validation, and achievement—regardless of the relationship's quality.

This chapter challenges that framework.

Not to dismiss partnership—but to decenter it.

Agility moves the partnership away from the center and restores alignment as the organizing principle.

Decentering Without Detaching

Decentering partnership does not mean rejecting intimacy, connection, or desire. It means removing partnership from its role as an identity anchor.

When partnership is treated as optional rather than essential, something powerful happens:

- Choice replaces urgency.
- Discernment replaces fear.
- Self-trust replaces performance.

Decentering allows women to remain open without becoming dependent. It restores agency without closing the door to love.

Agility lives in this balance.

Why Requirement Creates Distortion

When a partnership is required, tolerance increases. Red flags are downplayed, misalignment is minimized, and peace is postponed.

Requirements create pressure, and pressure distorts judgment. Decisions become reactive rather than reflective. Fear begins to drive accommodation.

Agility relieves pressure by restoring agency. When partnership is no longer necessary, clarity becomes possible.

Optionality Is Power

In leadership and systems design, optionality builds resilience. Well-functioning systems are not dependent on a single outcome. They adapt.

Human lives work the same way. When partnership is optional:

- Loneliness loses leverage.
- Scarcity loses influence.
- Clarity becomes accessible.

Optionality does not close doors.

It clarifies which doors are worth opening.

Agility recognizes that freedom expands choice rather than causing isolation.

A Full Life Is Not a Placeholder

A life rich in purpose, connection, creativity, and meaning is not a waiting room for partnership. It is the foundation.

When women build lives that are already full, the following elements come into play:

- Partnership becomes additive rather than compensatory.
- Desire becomes discerning, not desperate.
- Time becomes an ally, not a threat.

Agility honors fullness as strength, not as consolation. A full life does not compete with partnership. It prevents settling for less.

Redefining Success

Success in later life is not defined by proximity to others. It is defined as:

- Alignment.
- Peace.
- Integrity.

- Agency.
- Joy.

Partnership may support these outcomes—but it is not the only path to achieving them.

Agility reframes success as internal coherence rather than external validation.

Freedom from the Urgency Narrative

The urgency narrative emphasizes:

- Time is limited.
- Opportunities are diminishing.
- Compromise becomes essential.

This narrative thrives on fear and scarcity. It pressures women to move faster, settle sooner, and lower their standards.

Agility dissolves urgency by anchoring worth within.

Time does not diminish worth.

Age does not diminish value.

Choice does not require panic.

Vision: Partnership as Choice

Imagine a partnership approached without pressure.

Connection originates from curiosity rather than necessity. Commitment develops from alignment rather than fear. Boundaries are respected rather than negotiated away.

This is not idealism.

It is a possibility grounded in clarity.

Agility enables women to engage in partnerships as equals rather than as applicants.

When Partnership Comes, It Must Add

Optionality elevates the standard. A true partnership should:

- Enrich your life.
- Safeguard your peace.
- Honor your autonomy.
- Divide responsibilities.

Anything short of this isn't a partnership; it's merely proximity.

Agility rejects proximity masquerading as connection.

The Agile Reframe

An agile woman does not ask:
"How do I secure a partnership?"
She asks,
"What aligns with the life I have built?"
This shift changes everything—how she chooses, waits, and walks away.

Claiming the Future

The future is not defined by who arrives.

It is defined by how you live.

When a partnership is optional:

- Joy becomes present, not postponed.
- Self-worth becomes stable.
- Choice becomes intentional.

Agility empowers women to move forward without apology—open, grounded, and free-spirited.

CHAPTER 13

Building a Full Life Without Waiting

Waiting is one of the most socially ingrained habits that adults carry into later life.

Waiting to be chosen.

Waiting for a partnership.

Waiting for permission to begin.

Waiting is rarely described simply as waiting. Instead, it is framed as patience, practicality, realism, or hope. Over time, however, quiet waiting can turn into deferral—delaying life itself, a delay often justified by both women and men as a sign of maturity.

This chapter dismantles the belief that fulfillment is conditional and replaces it with agency, expansion, and self-direction.

Agility reorganizes life around intention rather than anticipation.

Waiting Is Not Neutral

Waiting feels passive, yet it carries active consequences. When women postpone experiences in anticipation of partnership, they unintentionally narrow their lives. Time passes. Curiosity dims. Confidence stagnates. What begins as patience slowly turns into inertia.

This erosion is subtle, not signaling dissatisfaction but rather appearing practical. Common thoughts that arise include:

"That would be better later."

"That can wait."

"I'll do that when..."

Agility reframes waiting as a decision—one that can be revisited, revised, and released.

Activity That Feels Like Movement—But Isn't

There is a modern form of waiting that often goes unnoticed because it looks active. It involves staying informed, vocal, and engaged. People spend hours commenting, reacting, posting, and consuming content, especially on topics such as dating, relationships, and cultural issues. In this mode, expression replaces movement, and validation replaces progress.

None of this is inherently wrong, but it is not the same as building a life.

When energy is continuously discharged through commentary rather than directed toward learning, creating, or expanding, it creates the illusion of participation while quietly postponing growth. The nervous system remains activated. The story repeats. Time passes. What is missing is movement—experiences that stretch capacity, deepen self-trust, and generate evidence rather than opinion.

Expression without movement can become a holding pattern. When frustration is repeatedly released without being converted into action, women remain emotionally busy yet structurally unchanged. Agility does not suppress the voice—it asks where energy is going.

Agility recognizes the difference between having a voice and having a trajectory. One releases pressure. The other changes outcomes.

A Life Lived Later Is Still a Life Lived Smaller

Many individuals secretly believe that meaningful experiences should be shared, so they often wait to share them until the "right" person appears. Common shared experiences that are postponed include:

- Travel.
- Exploration.
- Learning.
- Expansion.

The desire to share is human.

The delay is costly.

A life deferred does not preserve meaning—it diminishes momentum. Experiences that could have strengthened confidence and self-trust are replaced with speculation and longing.

A full life does not compete with partnership. It strengthens it.

A Common Observation

Over the years, it is not uncommon to meet men and women who have never traveled outside their home state, not because of limitations but because they have been waiting.

They are awaiting the right person to accompany them on their journey, seeking companionship to support their exploration, and hoping that someone else will lead the initiative to broaden their horizons.

What becomes clear is this:

Waiting rarely produces readiness.

Movement does.

Life does not expand in anticipation.

It expands in action.

Agility favors action—not recklessness, but engagement.

Education as Expansion

A full life is not built on experience alone—it is built on understanding.

Education in later life is not about credentials or status. It is about curiosity. It is about learning beyond what is familiar—cultures, ideas, histories, systems, and perspectives that challenge and expand our view of the world.

Women who continue to educate themselves—formally or informally—develop sharper discernment. They gain the language to articulate their experiences and become less reliant on others to define meaning, direction, or possibilities.

Education is the movement of the mind.
And movement, in any form, disrupts stagnation.

Agility thrives where learning persists.

Momentum Creates Confidence

In leadership and in life, momentum brings clarity. When women move through travel, learning, engagement, and exploration, they:

- Build confidence independent of validation.
- Expand identity beyond relational roles.
- Refine preferences through lived experience.
- Strengthen presence and self-trust.

Momentum reduces fear by replacing imagination with evidence.

Agility prioritizes momentum over delay.

Partnership Is Enhanced, Not Threatened, by Fullness

A common fear is that living fully alone may diminish the desire for partnership.

The opposite is often true.

A full, educated, and engaged life:

- Clarifies standards.
- Reduces tolerance for misalignment.
- Strengthens boundaries.
- Attracts alignment rather than urgency.

A partnership does not create fullness. Fullness clarifies a partnership.

Agility understands that expansion strengthens choice.

Letting Go of Conditional Living

Conditional living is a way of life in which acceptance or support depends on specific conditions being met:

- "When I meet someone, I'll…"
- "That would be better with a partner."
- "I'll wait until…"

These conditions quietly limit life.

Agility dismantles conditionality.

Joy does not require a witness.

Learning does not require permission.

Expansion does not require company.

Living fully is not an abandonment of partnership—it is preparation for it.

Designing a Life That Includes—but Does Not Depend on—Partnership

An empowered life is built intentionally rather than delayed. It includes:

- Purpose.
- Community.
- Learning.
- Exploration.
- Contribution.
- Rest.
- Pleasure.

Partnership, if it arrives, is an addition—not a foundation.

Agility builds a life that stands on its own.

The Agile Reframe

An agile woman does not ask:

"Who will I do this with?"

She asks,

"What kind of life am I building now?"

That question restores momentum, confidence, and a sense of agency.

Claiming Expansion

Expansion is a deliberate choice. It signifies actively seeking knowledge despite the temptation of comfort leading to complacency. It entails valuing curiosity over indifference and demonstrates a commitment to growth without assurances.

Agility gives women permission to live fully—now.

Not later.

Not conditionally.

Not eventually.

Now.

CHAPTER 14

If He Comes, He Must Add

By this point in the journey, something fundamental has changed.

You are no longer searching for possibilities.

You are no longer negotiating alignment.

You are no longer organizing your life around anticipation.

You are standing in clarity.

This chapter begins the crescendo by stating a simple, non-negotiable truth.

If a partner enters your life now, he must add to it.

This is not a demand.

It is not rigidity.

It is not defensiveness.

It is discernment gained through experience.

Addition Is the Baseline

Addition is not extravagance.

It is not perfection.

It is not constant ease.

Addition means your life functions better—not harder—because of the relationship.

A partner must add:

- Stability, not volatility.
- Effort, not excuses.
- Presence, not proximity.
- Respect, not tolerance.
- Peace, not management.

Anything less is subtraction.

Agility makes this distinction clear. There is no debate about when subtraction becomes visible.

Subtraction Is Often Quiet

Subtraction does not always announce itself as harm. It rarely arrives as conflict. More often, it appears as subtle friction—small compromises that accumulate quietly.

Subtraction is shown as:

- Explaining your needs repeatedly without behavioral change.
- Feeling relief when communication finally arrives.
- Managing your emotional tone to avoid disruption.
- Adjusting expectations downward to preserve harmony.
- Feeling responsible for sustaining momentum.
- Maintaining emotional vigilance even during calm.

None of these moments appears dramatic, which is why they are readily dismissible. However, subtraction is not measured by intensity. It is measured by erosion.

Agility acknowledges when a relationship gradually diminishes one's life, even if it does not overtly cause harm.

If something consistently requires you to compensate, recalibrate, or self-monitor, it does not add value.

It subtracts.

And over time, subtraction costs peace.

Why Addition Matters More Later in Life

In early life, relationships often form through shared struggles, such as building careers, raising families, and navigating uncertainty.

Later in life, the work is already complete.

You are not building from scratch.

You are integrating.

Integration requires compatibility at the following levels:

- Daily living.
- Emotional regulation.
- Communication patterns.
- Values and priorities.

A partner must be able to step into a fully formed life without disrupting its foundation.

At this stage, there is no margin for unnecessary erosion. Addition becomes the measure because the protection of peace is essential—not optional.

What "Adding" Actually Looks Like

Addition is observable. It is not abstract. It manifests as:

- Consistent communication that does not require monitoring.
- Follow-through without prompting.
- Shared responsibility for sustaining connection.
- Emotional availability paired with accountability.
- Willingness to adjust—not dominate— habits and routines.

Addition does not require persuasion.

It does not improve with patience.

It is offered freely, or it is absent.

The End of Justification

One of the clearest signs of growth is the end of justification.

You no longer explain why something should be acceptable.

You no longer rationalize misalignment.

You no longer negotiate yourself into discomfort.

Agility has done its work.

At this stage, clarity is quiet and decisive.

There is no emotional argument.

There is no internal debate.

There is recognition.

Standards as Self-Respect, Not Defense

Standards are often mischaracterized as barriers.

In reality, standards are structured. They do not exist to keep people out. They exist to ensure compatibility.

An agile woman does not defend her standards.

She does not justify them.

120

She does not soften them to appear flexible.

She lives by them.

Standards are not ultimatums.

They are filters.

Effort Is Not a Burden

A common myth is that requiring effort is the same as demanding.

Effort does not constitute a burden for an individual who is aligned.

It is a natural expression of interest.

When effort feels heavy, inconsistent, or transactional, alignment is lacking.

Agility means noticing the difference without debate.

No More Auditions

The crescendo begins when the auditions end. You are no longer proving:

- Your worth.
- Your flexibility.

- Your patience.
- Your emotional availability.

You are no longer adjusting to be selected.

You are evaluating fit.

This is not arrogance.

It is readiness.

Auditions are associated with uncertainty.

Clarity ends them.

Partnership as Enhancement

Partnership at this stage acts as an enhancement, improving:

- How you move through the world.
- How you experience joy.
- How you manage stress.
- How you feel in your body and mind.

If a relationship requires you to brace yourself rather than relax, it is not conducive to growth.

If a relationship increases vigilance rather than ease, it is not additive.

Agility teaches the body to recognize alignment before the mind rationalizes misalignment.

The Agile Reframe

An agile woman does not ask:

"Can I make this work?"

She asks,

"Does this work with who I am now?"

That question is the threshold.

Standing Firm Without Hardness

The beginning of the crescendo is not loud.

It is grounded.

You are not hardened.

You are not closed.

You are not inflexible.

You are clear.

And clarity is the most generous gift you can give yourself—and anyone who enters your life.

When addition becomes the baseline, urgency loses its grip.

You no longer rush to secure.

You no longer negotiate alignment.

You no longer confuse effort with interest.

What follows is not waiting.

It is calm.

Calm is the state in which discernment is steady, and decisions are not swayed by fear, urgency, or perceived scarcity.

From here, the question is no longer who might come.

The question is whether urgency has any place at all.

That is where the next shift begins.

CHAPTER 15

Aging Is Not the Emergency... Desperation Is

Urgency has quietly influenced women's decisions for far too long.

It whispers that time is running out.

That opportunity is shrinking.

That compromise is necessary.

Urgency rarely announces itself as fear. More often, it appears as practicality, realism, or the belief that this may be as good as it gets. Underlying it all is the same pressure: Decide quickly or lose your chance.

This chapter aims to dismantle that voice.

Not by denying desire.

Not by dismissing longing.

But by restoring perspective.

Where Urgency Comes From

Urgency does not originate within you.

Urgency is learned.

Women have been taught—explicitly and implicitly—that time is a threat, that desirability diminishes, and that partnership is a narrowing window rather than an evolving choice.

These messages accumulate over decades, reinforced by the media, peers, cultural narratives, and even well-meaning advice.

Urgency is not intuition.

It is conditioning.

When women internalize urgency, they begin to interpret normal uncertainty as danger and healthy pacing as risky. Desire becomes compressed by fear, and choice becomes reactive rather than intentional.

Agility begins when women recognize urgency as an inherited narrative rather than a personal truth.

Urgency Distorts Judgment

In every system—emotional, organizational, or relational—urgency narrows one's vision.

It compresses timelines.

It lowers standards.

It prioritizes action over alignment.

Urgency creates movement, not clarity. What it produces is pressure—pressure that rewards speed over discernment and proximity over compatibility. In dating, urgency often pushes women to:

- Over-invest prematurely.
- Rationalize misalignment.
- Silence intuition.
- Accept ambiguity as inevitability.

Agility restores perspective by slowing decision-making without halting progress.

Calm is not hesitation.

It is discernment.

Aging Is Not a Crisis

Aging is often framed as a decline.

In reality, aging constitutes an accumulation of insight, resilience, discernment, and self-knowledge. What diminishes over time is not the capacity for connection but the tolerance for dysfunction. With advancing age, individuals typically experience:

- Improved pattern recognition.
- More defined boundaries.
- Greater self-trust.
- Reduced appetite for emotional labor without reciprocal return.

The idea that love fades with age is not biological.

It is cultural.

Agility rejects the narrative that frames maturity as a deadline rather than an advantage.

Aging Is Not a Crisis

Why Desperation Is the Real Risk

Desperation causes imbalance well before a relationship starts. It leads to:

- Over-investment.
- Premature commitments.
- Erosion of boundaries.
- Self-silencing.
- Settling for less.

Desperation is not about seeking love.

It is about fearing absence.

When fear enters decision-making, clarity leaves.

Agility neutralizes fear by anchoring worth internally. When worth is stable, urgency loses its power.

Time as an Ally, Not an Enemy

When time is treated as an enemy, every decision becomes reactive.

When time is viewed as an ally, patience becomes strength.

In well-designed systems, time is not a liability; it serves as a diagnostic instrument. Time stress-tests stability, exposing weak integrations, faulty assumptions, and unsustainable designs.

Speed conceals flaws.

Time exposes them.

Relationships work the same way.

What cannot withstand the test of time cannot sustain a partnership.

An agile woman recognizes that rushing rarely yields the outcome she seeks, but clarity often does.

Time reveals.

Time refines.

Time filters.

Urgency interrupts this process.

Agility trusts it.

Urgency and the Myth of the Last Chance

The "last chance" narrative is among the most damaging myths in later-life dating. It implies:

- This is the final opportunity.
- Standards must be lowered.
- Decisions must be made more quickly.

This narrative does not hold.

Connection does not expire.

Compatibility does not fade with age.

What fades is tolerance for misalignment.

Agility replaces "last chance" thinking with right-fit thinking.

What is aligned does not require panic.

Slowness as Emotional Intelligence

Slowness is often mistaken for hesitation, but it reflects careful discernment. It enables:

- Observation without projection.
- Connection without pressure.
- Choice without fear.

Agility values pacing because it preserves peace. It allows patterns to emerge without imposing outcomes.

What is meant to align will stand the test of time.

Letting the Nervous System Settle

Much of the urgency resides within the nervous system.

Before the mind forms conclusions, the body reacts—registering tension, shallow breathing, restlessness, and a sharp focus on outcomes. These sensations are often mistaken for intuition, though they signal activation.

Agility invites regulation.

When the nervous system settles, clarity returns. Decisions made from regulation are quieter, more grounded, and less reactive.

Calm restores access to wisdom.

Choosing Calm Over Collapse

Calm is often misunderstood.

It is not indifference.

It is not disengagement.

It is not emotional distance.

Calm is stability.

Choosing calm means:

- No longer reacting to absence.
- No longer seeking reassurance.
- No longer making decisions out of fear.

Calm creates space for aligned connections to emerge—connections that do not require urgency to maintain.

The Shift That Follows Clarity

Once clarity is established—as reinforced in the previous chapter—urgency no longer has a place to land.

You are no longer rushing to secure.

You are no longer negotiating alignment.

You are no longer measuring yourself against the clock.

Urgency diminishes not due to a cessation of desire for connection but because the fear of its absence has been relinquished.

The Agile Reframe

An agile woman does not ask:
"What if this is my last chance?"
She asks,
"What aligns with my life, my values, and my peace?"
That question dissolves urgency.

Living Beyond the Clock

Life does not move on a deadline.
Love does not arrive on a schedule.
When urgency dissolves, presence expands.
Agility allows women to live fully—without racing toward an imagined finish line.
Not driven.

134

Not pressured.

Not compromised.

Present.

Reflection Questions (Chapter 15)

1. Where do I feel pressure that isn't actually mine?
2. How does my body respond when urgency appears?
3. What would it feel like to trust timing rather than fight it?
4. What changes when I choose calm over speed?

CHAPTER 16

Agility Is the New Attraction

Attraction changes as wisdom deepens.

What once drew attention—intensity, pursuit, validation—loses its power. In its place, something steadier emerges: presence, clarity, and ease. What attracts now is not emotional charge or momentum but coherence.

Agility is not something you perform.

It is something you become.

This chapter is not about how to attract.

It is about how attraction reorganizes when you are no longer negotiating from a place of fear.

Attraction Moves Toward Stability

At this stage, attraction shifts from excitement to harmony. It is influenced by the following:

- Managing emotions.
- Believing in oneself.
- Being consistent.
- Staying grounded.
- Maintaining inner clarity.

Stability is no longer mistaken for boredom. It is recognized as a capacity.

Agility signals stability—and stability is deeply attractive because it feels safe without being dull and is alive without being chaotic.

This attraction is quieter yet more powerful.

It does not spike.

It sustains.

What No Longer Attracts

As agility integrates, attraction becomes more refined. What was once compelling now seems costly. Intensity without stability, mystery without follow-through, chemistry without consistency, and desire without emotional safety are evident.

Agility does not reject desire—it matures it.

What no longer attracts is not wrong.

It is simply outgrown.

This shift is not a loss.

It is discernment.

Clarity Is Magnetic

Clarity reduces noise.

When a woman is self-aware of her identity, values, and approach to engaging with the world, she no longer sends mixed signals. There are no longer pursuits, explanations, emotional over-involvement, or a need to be understood at all costs.

Clarity does not persuade.

It invites.

Individuals are drawn to clarity not because it persuades them, but because it is easy to read. It remains consistent and does not bend or distort itself to fit confusion.

Agility eliminates static from the connection.

The Power of Not Needing to Convince

One of the most appealing aspects is the absence of persuasion.

Agile women do not convince others of their worth, flexibility, or desirability. They do not over-communicate their intentions. They do not manage outcomes or audition for approval.

Their presence speaks.

Attraction is directed toward that which is already established because established energy does not require selection. It signifies a state of fulfillment rather than lack.

Agility replaces explanation with embodiment.

Agility as Emotional Gravity

In physics, gravity is not associated with effort; it depends exclusively on mass.

Agility carries emotional weight. It draws in what is aligned and repels what is not, without resistance. There is no force, argument, or persuasion—only truth.

This is not detachment.

It is discernment embodied.

Agility does not pull.

It does not chase.

It does not harden.

It simply exists—and alignment responds.

How Agility Is Experienced by Others

Agility isn't something that is announced; it is experienced as:

- Calm confidence.
- Emotional steadiness.
- Clear boundaries.
- An unforced, natural presence.

People do not sense judgment.

They do not feel controlled.

They do not feel pressured.

They feel secure enough to be authentic.

Such genuine presence is uncommon.

And that rarity draws others in.

Ease as the New Chemistry

Chemistry built on tension ultimately depletes; ease lasts longer. This kind of ease manifests as:

- Mutual effort without the need for negotiation.
- Silence that does not provoke anxiety.
- Accepting differences without defensiveness.
- Being present without ease as compatibility, rather than boredom.

What might have previously been considered as "not enough spark" is now recognized as desire combined with safety. Ease does not mean a lack of passion; rather, it is passion expressed without chaos.

Attraction Without Urgency

Urgency distorts attraction. When urgency fades, attraction becomes clearer. It is no longer driven by fear, scarcity, or projection, nor does it seek premature reassurance or certainty.

Agility allows attraction to unfold naturally— without pressure or pursuit.

What is aligned does not require acceleration. What is sustainable does not fear time.

Wanting Love Without Losing Yourself

It is important to state this clearly: the desire for a beautiful, healthy relationship is part of human nature.

Women seek partnerships that are stable, mutually respectful, and emotionally safe. They want shared laughter, companionship, intimacy, and personal growth. Their aspiration is for love that enhances life, not complicates it.

Wanting this does not imply that a woman is weak.

It simply reflects a woman's humanity.

The difference now is not the desire for love but the unwillingness to sacrifice oneself, peace, and dignity in its pursuit.

True agility balances truth and desire.

Embodiment Over Strategy

Agility is not a dating technique; it is an internal disposition.

It manifests in one's manner of speaking.

It appears in the way pauses are taken.

It reveals itself in how one listens and in the choices one makes.

This quality cannot be simulated, because it is rooted in self-trust.

Attraction is a consequence of embodiment rather than exertion.

Presence surpasses any performative act in effectiveness.

Being Seen Without Performing

When performance dissolves, authenticity emerges.

Agility allows you to be seen without adjustment, to connect without management, and to exist without explanation.

You no longer curate yourself for palatability.

This is the deepest form of attraction:

Recognition without effort.

The Agile Reframe

An agile woman does not ask:

"How do I attract?"

She asks:

"How do I live in alignment?"

Attraction becomes a byproduct, not a goal.

Arriving at Yourself

At this point, you are no longer seeking signals.

You are the signal.

Your life mirrors your values.

Your boundaries reflect your clarity.

Your presence reflects your peace.

Agility has become your identity.

Closing the Circle

This chapter is not an ending; rather, it marks a return.

A return to oneself.

A return to ease.

A return to discernment without fear.

Attraction is guided by truth, and truth is inherently magnetic.

CONCLUSION

Moving Forward Without Apology

At this point, a state of calm has been established, marked by the absence of desire, openness, or hope. The sense of urgency has eased.

You are no longer rushing toward an outcome or negotiating out of fear. You are no longer measuring your worth by proximity, attention, potential, or timing. You are no longer clarifying your standards, diminishing your clarity, or interpreting inconsistency as something to manage.

You have acquired the ability to discern patterns with clarity.

You have learned to respect peace without guilt.

You have understood how to act with purpose rather than merely react.

This is agility.

Agility as a Way of Being

Agility is not detachment; it is discernment in motion. It embodies the capacity to remain receptive without overextending oneself, to make choices without performative acts, and to disengage without becoming rigid. It manifests as a form of clarity that does not seek to announce itself overtly, and as confidence that does not require constant reinforcement.

Agility isn't loud or flashy; it's calm and confident. It is demonstrated through attentive listening, deliberate pauses, well-considered decisions, and selective pursuits.

You are no longer focused on managing perceptions or outcomes.

You are living in authentic alignment.

Attraction Reconsidered

Agility has transformed how attraction works in your life. You no longer confuse intensity with intimacy or urgency with genuine interest. Instead, you recognize that what attracts you now is not effort, availability, or emotional intensity, but consistency.

Presence now supplants pursuit.

Ease replaces tension.

Stability has replaced uncertainty.

You are no longer trying to be magnetic.

You are magnetic because you are grounded.

Agility does not chase attraction; it allows attraction to align with the truth.

Wanting Love, Without Losing Yourself

Most women desire a beautiful, healthy relationship, and that has never been contested. What has shifted is the refusal to sacrifice dignity, peace, or identity for it. There's now an understanding that love chosen with clarity is fundamentally different from love driven by fear.

You realize that seeking a partnership doesn't need to be urgent.

Desire does not require self-abandonment.

Openness doesn't mean overextending oneself.

Agility allows you to hold both desire and self-respect simultaneously.

What You Now Understand

You realize that:

- Availability does not equal readiness.
- Effort demonstrates intent.
- Consistency reflects genuine interest.
- Peace indicates alignment.
- Time itself isn't the enemy— misalignment is.

You recognize that not every situation requires a response, not every opportunity should be pursued, and not every connection needs to endure. More importantly, you understand that you don't need to justify your standards to uphold them.

Sovereignty Without Apology

Agility does not seek permission.

It does not require justification.

It refrains from argument.

It merely proceeds.

If partnership comes, let it come as an addition—not a correction. Let it meet you where you are now, not where you were once taught to wait. Let it honor the life you have built, the clarity you have earned, and the peace you safeguard. If it does not come, let your life remain rich—with purpose, connection, curiosity, learning, contribution, and joy.

If partnership arrives, welcome it as an enhancement—not a correction. Let it align with your current state, not with where you were once told to wait. Ensure it honors the life you've created, the clarity you've gained, and the peace you maintain. If it doesn't arrive, let your life continue to thrive—filled with purpose, connection, curiosity, learning, contribution, and joy.

Not as a consolation.

As a choice.

The Final Integration

This is not a resignation; it is an act of self-leadership. You are not merely awaiting circumstances; instead, you are actively engaging in life.

Agility has transitioned from being a mere practice to becoming an integral part of your essence. From a grounded, clear, and embodied state, everything that presents itself will be in alignment—or you will opt not to pursue it.

Either way, you advance fully and intact.

On Agility and Self-Leadership

My understanding of agility doesn't stem from dating; rather, it originates from the fields of technology and leadership. In technology, agility is not merely about speed. It is the ability to respond effectively without compromise, to evaluate circumstances accurately, to adapt as conditions evolve, and to safeguard fundamental principles while modifying strategies. Inflexible systems tend to fail, and those that neglect data fail even more rapidly.

I've spent years in environments where adaptability was crucial, and clinging to outdated methods carried real risks. In such settings, the ability to pivot isn't a sign of weakness but of sound decision-making.

Teams that couldn't adapt weren't necessarily more principled; they were more fragile. Successful systems weren't those that resisted change but those that learned to adapt while preserving their core integrity.

Over time, I recognized the parallel. Relationships, like systems, operate within a landscape of ever-changing conditions. Context shifts, capacity varies, and what works in one season may not in another. What was once perceived as harmonious can subtly evolve into misalignment.

Growth is inherently nonlinear, and wisdom is seldom acquired without experience. Nevertheless, in the realm of relationships, there is a prevalent belief that endurance is a virtue and discomfort a testament to commitment, even when the system in question is clearly deteriorating. This assumption, however, is fundamentally flawed.

A relationship, like any complex system, needs feedback, adjustments, and accountability.

Without these, it can't deepen and may deteriorate.

I have also experienced partnership and marriage firsthand—more than once. These experiences were genuine, committed, and educational. They demonstrated that proximity alone does not ensure alignment; that longevity does not inherently signify health; and that maintaining functionality requires more than mere endurance. From these experiences, one thing became clear: commitment without flexibility ultimately fails.

This book is rooted in my active involvement with leadership, systems, relationships, and self-awareness. The lessons are based on participation, reflection, and recalibration, not avoidance. They arise from the intersection of theory and real-world experience, where intent aligns with impact, and clarity takes precedence over narrative.

The principles I rely on in professional environments remain consistent: observing patterns, responding to data, correcting courses early, and safeguarding what matters most. 'Agility Over 50' summarizes these lessons, applying the same discernment used in leadership and technology to our emotional experiences.

Agility encourages us to recognize when to iterate, maintain stability, or disengage, all while avoiding collapse, bitterness, or self-erasure. This approach challenges the assumption that staying in a situation always signifies strength and that leaving signifies failure. Most importantly, this endeavor centers on respecting growth. Growth does not imply prior failure; rather, it signifies that we have learned.

Agility also empowers us to retain that knowledge for future reference—without apology, without urgency, and without forsaking our integrity. It supports staying open-minded without naivety, discerning without becoming rigid, and preserving hope without resorting to superficial gestures.

That constitutes the essence of this book.

And it is the pursuit I consistently exemplify.